THE THERAPIST'S TRIUMPH: Therapist Success Blueprint: Build, Scale, Succeed!

Nelda A. Crane

Copyright ©

Table of contents

Chapter 1
Introduction

Chapter 2
The Foundation of a Therapist

Chapter 3
Discovering the Path of Healing

Chapter 4
Understanding human psychology

Chapter 5
Building Therapeutic Relationships

- Tools of Transformation: Therapeutic Approaches and Techniques
- Cultural Competence and Sensitivity
- Boundaries and Ethical Considerations

Chapter 6
Life Renovation

- Hopelessness to Healing
- Rebuilding Broken Relationships
- Overcoming Trauma and Reclaiming Life
- Personal Growth and Resilience
- Financial benefits

Conclusion

- Acknowledgments

CHAPTER 1

INTRODUCTION

The journey

The role of a therapist is important in the sacred region of the human mind, where emotions ebb and flow like a vast ocean. It is a monumental journey through the depths of human experience in pursuit of peace, understanding, and hope for those in need. Welcome to "The Therapist Triumph," an amazing narrative about empathy, tenacity, and the magical power of healing.

Within these pages, we embark on a one-of-a-kind trip into the life of a therapist, complete with ups and downs along the route to understanding, acceptance, and transformation. It's a narrative of kindness, wisdom, and the indomitable spirit that penetrates every treatment session.

As we delve deeper into their inner world, we see their own metamorphosis as they face their weaknesses, accept self-care, and find the strength to continue illuminating the path of healing.

"The Therapist Triumph" invites you to accompany us on an astonishing journey that challenges assumptions, inspires compassion, and reminds us of the tenacity of the human spirit. It honors the therapist's accomplishment, dedication to the well-being of others, and the extraordinary impact they have on the lives they touch.

As we embark on this soul-stirring trip, prepare to be interested, enlightened, and moved. Let us discover the immense triumph that lives within the hearts and minds of those who embark on this magnificent journey with us as we uncover the transformative power of therapy.

Goal of the book

This book is to help therapist exceptionally professional, adding to their personal growth and financial success. The introduction sets the stage for an engaging exploration of the therapist's journey, showcasing the potential for both personal fulfillment and financial abundance in the realm of therapy. This book focuses on a therapist's foundation - nurturing compassion, empathy, and healing

About the author

Nelda A. Crane is a renowned author and a passionate advocate for mental health and personal growth. With a wealth of experience in the field of therapy and counseling, Nelda brings a unique perspective to her writing, drawing from her years of professional practice and dedication to helping others.

Her expertise lies in working with individuals who have experienced various forms of trauma and guiding them towards healing and transformation.

Throughout her career, Nelda has touched the lives of countless clients, helping them navigate through their challenges and discover their inner strength. Her empathetic approach, combined with her deep understanding of human psychology, has earned her recognition as a trusted therapist and mentor.

In addition to her clinical work, Nelda is an avid writer who is committed to sharing her knowledge and insights with a wider audience. Her book, "Therapist Triumph," delves into the triumphs and struggles faced by therapists in their professional journeys. Drawing from her own experiences and those of her colleagues, Nelda provides valuable guidance and inspiration for therapists seeking personal and professional fulfillment.

Nelda's writing style is characterized by a compassionate and relatable tone, making complex psychological concepts accessible to readers from all walks of life. Her dedication to promoting mental health awareness and destigmatizing therapy shines through in her writing, as she encourages readers to embrace their own journeys of self-discovery and growth.

When she's not writing or working with clients, Nelda enjoys spending time in nature, practicing mindfulness, and engaging in creative pursuits. She also frequently presents at conferences and conducts workshops, sharing her expertise with fellow professionals and aspiring therapists.

"Therapist Triumph" is Nelda A. Crane's first book, and it serves as a testament to her unwavering commitment to supporting the mental health community. Her words are a source of inspiration for both therapists and individuals seeking to understand the transformative power of therapy.

CHAPTER 2

A therapist's foundation

Therapists act as pillars of support in the enormous terrain of mental and emotional well-being, offering guidance and healing to those in need. "The Foundation of a Therapist" digs into the fundamental elements that shape these incredible people as they nurture the critical traits of compassion, empathy, and healing.

Within these pages, we embark on an enthralling journey into the heart and soul of a therapist. We delve into the formative experiences, personal growth, and unwavering dedication that served as the foundation for their extraordinary work. It exemplifies how powerful empathy and understanding can be in the lives of others.

"The Foundation of a Therapist" dives into the numerous aspects of their personal and professional development. We examine the educational foundations, rigorous training, and continual pursuit of knowledge that enable therapists to provide the best possible care. We witness their personal healing journeys as they confront their own vulnerabilities, paving the way for genuine connection and profound transformation.

In this book, we celebrate the artistry of therapy—the delicate balance of science and intuition that therapists utilize to navigate the complexities of the human mind. We investigate the intricate network of emotions, traumas, and personal histories that characterize their clients' life. Therapists, by their expert guidance, become change agents, creating a safe space for healing to flourish.

"The Foundation of a Therapist" encourages you to enter the brains of these committed professionals as they develop the qualities that will propel them to success. It demonstrates their unwavering commitment to the well-being of others, as well as the tremendous power of their job.

Join us on this interesting journey to learn more about the therapist's foundation, unwavering compassion, and one-of-a-kind capacity to promote recovery. Through these pages, we discover the distinct essence of a therapist—their ability to forge meaningful relationships, ignite transformation, and nourish the human spirit.

As we go on this trip, expect to be inspired, enlightened, and moved. Allow "The Foundation of a Therapist" to illuminate the path to knowledge, compassion, and healing—a must-read for aspiring therapists as well as those interested in the enormous effect of their mind.

A call to help

The first thing that comes to mind for a therapist when making a decision is that the profession is a call to help. It is the goal of a therapist to guide, transform, and heal people of various natures, cultures, and tribes. Being a shoulder that could always be relied on for comfort.

Professional and academic credentials

Welcome to "The Therapist Triumph," an intriguing look of empathy, resilience, and the extraordinary financial benefits of being a successful therapist.

In this book, we delve into the extraordinary journey of therapists who not only heal hearts and minds but also enjoy enormous financial success. We learn about therapy's transformative power, which not only brings serenity and understanding but also opens the door to financial success.

We observe the huge impact treatment has on individuals, families, and communities via our protagonist's experiences. We show how a therapist's extraordinary abilities and unwavering dedication can not only help lives but also result in substantial financial rewards.

"The Therapist Triumph" highlights the financial benefits of a flourishing therapeutic profession. We examine the approaches, ideas, and tried-and-true tactics that can propel therapists to exceptional success in their industry.

The keys to financial wealth can be found in the field of therapy, from acquiring a steady supply of customers to implementing effective marketing tactics.

Join us on this exciting adventure that combines the art of healing with the pursuit of financial success. Prepare to be blown away as we unveil the immense success and financial prospects that await those who choose a career as a professional and successful therapist.

In these pages, we invite you to discover the transformative power of therapy, not only for the enhancement of people's lives, but also for financial gain. "The Therapist Triumph" is your guide to achieving both personal and financial success in the fast-paced field of therapy.

Increasing therapeutic abilities

For any mental health practitioner or anybody interested in helping others, developing therapeutic skills is a valuable and continuing practice. When building therapeutic skills, consider the following essential steps and areas to concentrate on:

1. Education and Training: Get the education and training you need to become a mental health professional. This usually entails earning a relevant degree (such as psychology, counseling, or social work) and acquiring any certifications or licenses required in your state.

2. Theoretical Understanding: Become acquainted with various treatment techniques and theoretical frameworks. Cognitive-behavioral therapy (CBT), psychodynamic therapy,

humanistic therapy, and solution-focused short treatment are a few examples. To have a better awareness of various treatment techniques, read books, attend workshops, and take courses.

3. Clinical Supervision: Seek clinical supervision from a registered mental health practitioner with experience. Supervision allows you to discuss instances, get feedback, and get advice on therapeutic interventions. It allows you to reflect on your practice and improve your abilities.

4. Empathy and Active Listening: Practice empathy and active listening. These abilities include being fully present, carefully listening, and demonstrating true empathy and understanding to customers. This provides clients with a secure and supportive setting in which to share their thoughts and feelings.

5. Communication Skills: Improve your vocal and nonverbal communication skills. Learn to interact with clients in a straightforward, respectful, and aggressive manner. To demonstrate empathy and support, practice utilizing proper body language, tone of voice, and facial expressions.

6. Assessment and Diagnosis: Discover how to conduct comprehensive assessments and make reliable diagnoses. Learn about the diagnostic criteria for common mental health illnesses. To acquire relevant information, practice delivering assessment instruments and conducting interviews.

7. Treatment Planning: Learn how to create thorough treatment programs. Collaborate with clients to determine goals and appropriate actions based on their specific requirements. Understand evidence-based interventions and how to personalize them to specific clients.

8. Ethical and Legal Considerations: Keep up to date on ethical norms and legal restrictions that apply to your profession. Understand and follow the confidentiality, informed consent, and professional boundaries principles. When faced with an ethical quandary, seek supervision or guidance.

9. Self-awareness and self-care: Practice self-reflection and personal development. Acquaint yourself with your own biases, triggers, and limitations. Maintaining your own mental and emotional well-being through self-care activities will improve your ability to support others.

10. Continuing Education: Stay up to date on the newest mental health research, treatments, and developments. To broaden your knowledge and abilities, attend conferences, workshops, and seminars. To advance your professional development, seek regular supervision or counseling.

Keep in mind that learning therapeutic skills is a lifetime process. It takes time, practice, and a commitment to lifelong learning. In order to give the best possible care to those you serve, seek feedback from clients and colleagues, participate in self-reflection, and embrace chances for growth and development.

The importance of self care as a therapist

Self-care is particularly important for the rapists and mental health professionals due to the nature of their work. Here's why self-care is crucial for therapists:

Emotional Resilience: As a therapist, you are exposed to clients' emotional struggles, trauma, and difficult life situations. Providing empathetic support and holding space for others can be emotionally demanding. Engaging in self-care activities helps you maintain emotional resilience, preventing compassion fatigue and burnout.

Boundaries and Professionalism: Practicing self-care enables you to establish and maintain healthy boundaries with clients. It allows you to differentiate between your personal and professional life, ensuring that you have the necessary energy and focus to provide quality care without compromising your own well-being.

Personal Growth and Self-Reflection: Engaging in self-care activities promotes self-reflection, self-awareness, and personal growth. It allows you to continuously explore and process your own emotions, biases, and triggers, which can enhance your effectiveness as a therapist. Self-care activities such as therapy, supervision, or personal development workshops can support this process.

Role Modeling: Clients look to therapists as role models for healthy living and well-being. By prioritizing self-care, you set an example for your clients, demonstrating the importance of self-nurturing, self-compassion, and overall wellness. Your own self-care practices can inspire and empower clients to prioritize their own well-being.

Avoiding Therapist Burnout: Constantly supporting others can take a toll on your mental, emotional, and physical health. Neglecting self-care increases the risk of experiencing burnout, which can lead to decreased job satisfaction, impaired professional performance, and a compromised ability to provide effective therapy. Regular self-care helps prevent burnout and promotes longevity in your career.

1. Enhanced Therapeutic Presence: Engaging in self-care activities allows you to show up fully present and engaged in therapy sessions. When you take care of your own well-being, you can be more attuned to your clients' needs, respond empathetically, and provide quality care. It helps you maintain the energy, focus, and emotional availability required for effective therapy.

2. Stress Reduction and Personal Well-being: Self-care helps manage stress levels and promotes your own personal well-being. By engaging in activities that bring you joy, relaxation, and fulfillment, you can recharge and rejuvenate outside of your therapeutic

work. This helps maintain your own mental and emotional health, which ultimately benefits both you and your clients

Remember, self-care is not a luxury but a necessity for therapists. Prioritizing your own well-being allows you to be a more effective and compassionate practitioner, ensuring that you can continue to provide the best possible care for your clients over the long term

CHAPTER 3

DISCOVERING THE PATH OF HEALING

Discovering a career as a therapist can be a very rewarding and life-long adventure. It entails not only gaining knowledge and abilities, but also cultivating self-awareness and empathy. Here are some steps to aid you along the way:

Education and Training: First and foremost, receive a strong education in psychology, counseling, or a similar discipline. Pursue a degree or certification program that teaches you about human behavior, therapeutic procedures, and ethical practices. This foundation will provide you with the knowledge and resources you need to help your clients.

Clinical Experience: Look for ways to obtain hands-on experience in a clinical setting. Internships, supervised practice, or volunteering at counseling centers, hospitals, or mental health clinics could all be part of this. Working with a variety of people and presenting difficulties can extend your understanding and develop your therapeutic skills.

Personal Therapy: Engaging in one's personal therapy is an important part of the healing process for therapists. It enables you to investigate your own sensitivities, triggers, and unsolved issues, increasing your self-awareness and empathy. This technique will help you have a better grasp of the therapeutic path and the problems your clients may experience.

Continuing Education: Because healing is an ongoing process, you should look for chances for professional development and progress as a therapist. Attend workshops, conferences, and seminars to keep up with the most recent research, therapeutic techniques, and solutions. This ongoing education will improve your efficacy as a therapist and broaden your repertory of therapeutic practices.

Regular supervision or contact with competent therapists can provide vital guidance and support. Discussing cases, soliciting comments, and debating ethical quandaries with a trusted mentor or supervisor can help you get a better grasp of the therapeutic process and handle complicated challenges that may emerge in your practice.

Mindfulness and Self-Care: Make your personal self-care and well-being a priority. Participate in activities that encourage introspection, stress reduction, and relaxation. Mindfulness methods such as meditation or yoga can help you be present and in tune with your clients' needs while also preserving your own mental and emotional balance.

Understand the significance of cultural competence in your therapeutic work. Learn how culture, ethnicity, gender, and other social aspects affect clients' experiences and worldviews. To ensure that you can give effective and inclusive care to diverse populations, you should constantly educate yourself about different cultures and their distinctive healing methods.

Reflective Practice: Engage in self-evaluation and reflection on a regular basis to improve your efficacy as a therapist. Take into account your therapy approach, interventions, and the impact you have on your clients. To acquire insights and create improvements, solicit feedback from clients, coworkers, and supervisors.

Remember that the path of healing as a therapist is a lifelong journey of discovery and progress. Accept humility, keep an open mind, and be ready to change your approach as you learn and receive new insights. Your dedication to your own healing journey will improve your capacity to help and guide your clients on their own recovery journeys.

A Determined Change Advocate

As a therapist, being a passionate advocate for change may be a powerful and transforming strategy to assisting your clients. As a therapist, your primary purpose is to assist people on their path to growth, healing, and positive transformation. You may inspire and empower your clients to achieve important life changes by bringing your passion for change into your practice. Here are some important factors to consider:

Encourage your clients to participate actively in their therapy process. Assist them in recognizing their own skills, resources, and capacity for change. Give them the authority to make decisions, set goals, and take steps toward good change.

Consider therapy to be a constructive relationship between you and your clients. Create an open, respectful environment in which clients may express themselves and explore their goals for change. Engage in active listening and collaborate to build strategies that are in line with their objectives.

Optimism and Hope: Infuse sessions with optimism and hope. Assist clients in visualizing a future in which transformation is both attainable and practical. Highlight and applaud their accomplishments, no matter how minor. This can improve their confidence and enthusiasm to continue their transformational path.

Education and Awareness: Inform clients about the therapeutic process and change principles. Give them the knowledge and tools they need to comprehend their own ideas, feelings, and behaviors. Encourage self-reflection and introspection to help them become more self-aware.

Advocacy: Both within and outside of the treatment room, advocate for your clients' needs and rights. Assist them in navigating processes, gaining access to resources, and overcoming obstacles that may impede their advancement. Be their ally and encourage them to make the changes they want in their personal and social life.

Commit to your own growth and learning as a therapist as a passionate champion for change. Keep up with the most recent research, treatment techniques, and social challenges. Continuously broaden your knowledge and skills to better fulfill the different demands of your clientele.

Remember that being a passionate change advocate does not imply putting your own agenda on your clients. Instead, it entails leading and supporting individuals on their individual journey toward the desired goals. You may have a major impact as a therapist and inspire good shifts by creating a therapeutic space that appreciates their autonomy, strengths, and aspirations.

Putting the pieces together; from empathy to expertise

Before you can become an expert in your area as a therapist, you must first establish a firm foundation of empathy. Empathy is the foundation of the therapeutic connection and is essential for deeply understanding and relating with your clients. Here are several steps to go from empathy to expertise as a therapist:

Self-Reflection and Awareness: Start by becoming more self-aware and reflecting on your own experiences, biases, and beliefs. This self-reflection allows you to gain a better understanding of yourself, your emotions, and how they may affect your relationships with clients. Recognizing your own weaknesses allows you to create empathy and become more sensitive to your customers' experiences.

Active listening is an essential ability for every therapist. Active listening entails paying close attention to your clients and their verbal and nonverbal indications. Show your attentiveness by making eye contact, nodding, and making reflecting statements. Active listening allows you to comprehend your clients' points of view, emotions, and demands.

Cultivate Emotional Intelligence: Improve your emotional intelligence so that you can notice and understand your clients' feelings. Emotional intelligence entails skillfully perceiving, managing, and expressing emotions. You can improve your ability to empathize with your clients' circumstances and respond in a supportive and appropriate manner by mastering this skill.

Empathic Attunement is the ability to connect closely with customers and understand their subjective experiences. It entails putting oneself in their position and seeking to feel their emotions. Empathic attunement contributes to the development of rapport and trust, allowing clients to feel understood and affirmed.

Cultural Competence: Develop cultural competence by becoming acquainted with various cultures, backgrounds, and belief systems. Recognize and respect your clients' diversity, as cultural influences can have a huge impact on their experiences and worldviews. Being culturally competent allows you to give successful therapy while taking into account each client's unique needs and values.

Continuous Learning and Professional Development: In order to gain competence, it is necessary to engage in continual learning and professional development. Keep up to date on the most recent research, therapy strategies, and interventions in your profession. Attend courses, conferences, and seminars to broaden your knowledge and sharpen your therapeutic abilities.

Regular supervision and advice from qualified therapists or supervisors is recommended. They can help you negotiate challenging instances and enhance your knowledge by providing guidance, comments, and assistance. Supervision assists you in gaining new perspectives, identifying blind spots, and improving your therapeutic talents.

Remember that the road from empathy to expertise is an ongoing one that takes commitment and self-reflection. You can become a successful and compassionate therapist by building empathy and constantly improving your skills.

CHAPTER 4

Understanding human psychology

Understanding human psychology is critical for a therapist to properly help patients manage their ideas, feelings, and behaviors. Here are some crucial areas to explore as a therapist striving to understand human psychology:

Theoretical Frameworks: Learn about many psychological theories and techniques, including cognitive-behavioral therapy (CBT), psychodynamic theory, humanistic treatment, and others. These frameworks lay the groundwork for understanding how people think, feel, and act.

Developmental Psychology: Learn about human development across the lifespan. Understanding the physical, cognitive, social, and emotional changes that occur from infancy to adulthood is part of this. Recognize that people's psychological well-being is shaped by their experiences at various phases of life.

Emotional Regulation: Investigate how people regulate their emotions, deal with stress, and resolve problems. Understanding emotional states, their triggers, and the impact on behavior is critical in assisting clients in managing their emotional well-being.

Cognitive Processes: Investigate how humans perceive, interpret, and make sense of their surroundings. Recognize cognitive biases, automatic ideas, and how cognitive distortions affect mental health. This knowledge can be used to guide interventions that address negative thought patterns.

Attachment Theory: Discover attachment styles and how they affect relationships and well-being. Recognize the influence of early interactions on emotional development, as well as how attachment patterns may impair clients' current functioning.

Cultural and Social Influences: Recognize how cultural, social, and systemic elements influence people's thoughts, feelings, and behaviors. Recognize how cultural values, customs, and societal forces influence a person's psychological experiences.

Psychopathology: Become acquainted with the various psychological disorders and their diagnostic criteria as stated in the Diagnostic and Statistical Manual of Mental Disorders (DSM-5). Learn about the symptoms, causation, and evidence-based therapies for a variety of illnesses.

Therapeutic approaches: Learn about numerous therapeutic approaches and interventions that are specific to certain theoretical orientations. Learn how to use these strategies in practice to meet the needs and goals of your clients.

Self-respect and self-awareness: As a therapist, recognize the value of self-reflection and self-awareness. Engage in personal introspection and supervision on a regular basis to obtain insight into your own prejudices, values, and countertransference, as they might have an impact on your therapeutic practice.

Continual Learning: Because psychology is a constantly growing subject, keep up to date on current research and attend workshops, seminars, and conferences to increase your understanding and improve your skills as a therapist.

Remember that understanding human psychology is a lifelong endeavor, and each person you work with will bring their own set of experiences and issues. Being open-minded, compassionate, and inquisitive will assist you in forming a strong therapeutic bond and providing effective assistance to your clients.

Human Behavior Revealed

Unmasking human behavior as a therapist entails understanding the underlying elements that contribute to a person's ideas, feelings, and actions. It entails peeling back the layers of protective systems, prior experiences, and unconscious processes that influence a person's behavior. Here are some crucial points to consider as a therapist while deciphering human behavior:

Establishing rapport: It is critical to establish a solid therapeutic connection. Making the environment secure and trusting helps clients to open up and reveal their actual feelings and thoughts.

Active listening and observation: During treatment sessions, pay attentive attention to verbal and nonverbal cues. Pay close attention to what and how clients say it, as well as their body language, facial expressions, and tone of voice. These signs can reveal important information about their underlying feelings and motivations.

Empathy and perspective-taking: Attempt to comprehend the client's experiences from their perspective. Empathy enables you to connect with their feelings and gain a better understanding of their actions.

Exploring early life experiences: Childhood experiences, in particular, impact a person's ideas, coping strategies, and patterns of behavior. You can find underlying causes that lead to present behaviour by studying these events.

Identifying defense mechanisms: Defense mechanisms are unconscious techniques that people use to protect themselves from emotional anguish or discomfort. Denial, suppression, projection, and rationalization are all common defense tactics. Recognizing these mechanisms can aid in the discovery of buried emotions and underlying problems.

Recognizing patterns and themes: Examine a client's behavior, thoughts, and relationships for reoccurring patterns and themes. These patterns can reveal their core beliefs, unsolved conflicts, and unsatisfied needs.

Investigating unconscious processes: The unconscious mind has a huge influence on our actions. Unconscious intentions and conflicts can be revealed through techniques such as dream analysis, free association, and investigating symbolic meanings.

Cultural and social context: Consider how cultural and social elements influence a person's conduct. Cultural standards, societal expectations, and familial dynamics can all influence how people view and behave with others.

Self-reflection and countertransference: Consider your own reactions, feelings, and biases during therapy sessions. The therapist's emotional response to the client is referred to as countertransference, and it can reveal insights into the client's dynamics as well as provoke own unresolved difficulties.

Feedback and collaboration: Maintain an open and collaborative dialogue with clients. Encourage them to share their thoughts and observations on their own behavior and the counseling process. Collaborative exploration promotes self-awareness and behavioral change.

Unmasking human behavior is a difficult and ongoing process that necessitates a combination of therapeutic abilities, empathy, and comprehension. Each client must be treated with dignity, compassion, and an open mind, allowing them to reveal their actual selves and strive toward personal growth and healing.

Unlocking Personalities: Illuminating Theories

Exploring theories that provide insight on human behavior and attributes is part of Unlocking Personalities. Each perspective, from Freud's psychoanalytic theory to Jung's analytical psychology, offers distinct insights into the formation and evolution of personalities. These theories direct therapeutic actions and promote human development.

Cognitive Processes and Emotional Mastery in the Mind

Understanding the complex interplay between cognitive processes and emotional mastery is critical for supporting effective treatment and directing clients toward personal growth and well-being as a therapist. Cognitive processes are the mental operations involved in acquiring, processing, storing, and using knowledge, whereas emotional mastery is the development of emotional awareness and management.

Therapists can assist clients in identifying and challenging negative thought patterns that contribute to emotional suffering by understanding the relationship between cognition and emotion. Individuals can learn to reframe their thinking and acquire healthier perspectives using cognitive restructuring strategies, resulting in improved emotional well-being.

Furthermore, therapists trained in emotional mastery can help clients recognize and manage their emotions in healthy ways. Therapists empower clients to negotiate difficult situations, manage with stress, and build resilience through teaching emotional regulation skills.

Therapists can give clients with a holistic approach to mental health by merging understanding of cognitive processes and emotional skills. Therapists can help clients cultivate higher self-awareness, emotional intelligence, and overall psychological well-being by using individualized interventions and evidence-based strategies.

Unleashing Empathy: The Art of Deep Listening

It entails being fully present, understanding without passing judgment, and actively connecting with clients. Therapists create trust, validate experiences, and encourage clients to develop their own answers for growth and healing via thorough listening.

Human Behavior Revealed

It entails removing the layers of a person's ideas, feelings, and actions in order to understand the underlying motivations and patterns that drive their behavior. Encourage clients to expose their actual selves and examine the fundamental reasons of their problems by fostering a comfortable and nonjudgmental environment. Unmasking human behavior enables for in-depth reflection, self-awareness, and the possibility of good transformation. Assist individuals in gaining insights and developing healthier coping mechanisms, resulting in personal growth and improved well-being.

Unlocking Personalities: Illuminating Theories

As a therapist, you must employ a variety of theories to unlock and enlighten people. Psychodynamic, cognitive-behavioral, and humanistic techniques throw light on clients' inner workings, allowing them to better understand themselves. These ideas serve as frameworks for clients to explore their thoughts, feelings, and actions, helping them toward self-discovery, growth, and healing.

Cognitive Processes and Emotional Mastery in the Mind

I realize the importance of the mind and its cognitive processes in emotional mastery in therapy. Guide clients in developing healthy cognitive patterns by understanding how thoughts, beliefs, and interpretations shape emotions. We investigate and confront negative or distorted thinking via cognitive-behavioral approaches and mindfulness practices, encouraging emotional regulation and resilience. Therapy becomes a transforming journey of self-awareness, personal growth, and emotional well-being when cognitive processes are addressed and clients are empowered with effective coping techniques.

Chapter 5

Developing Therapeutic Relationships with Resilience

Building resilient therapeutic connections is essential for ensuring positive treatment outcomes and providing clients with effective support. The following are some fundamental principles and practices for developing and sustaining resilient therapeutic relationships:

Establishing trust and maintaining a secure environment are essential components of every therapy partnership. Clients must feel safe and comfortable when discussing their thoughts, feelings, and weaknesses. To develop a sense of safety and trust, therapists should display empathy, active listening, and nonjudgmental acceptance.

Authenticity and Genuineness: Being authentic and genuine allows therapists to connect with their clients on a deeper level. Authenticity entails being honest to oneself, being upfront about one's limitations, and being open to exploring the therapy process with others. When clients believe their therapist is true and authentic, they are more likely to engage and trust them.

Empathy and Understanding: Empathy is the ability to comprehend and share another person's feelings. Therapists should seek to comprehend their clients' experiences, viewpoints, and emotions, and then communicate that understanding through empathic answers. Empathy makes clients feel seen, heard, and validated, which leads to a stronger therapeutic bond.
 Decision-making: Encourage clients to make collaborative decisions in order to empower them and support their active engagement in the therapeutic process. Involve clients in goal-setting, intervention selection, and progress evaluation. This collaborative approach increases motivation and engagement by instilling a sense of ownership and responsibility.

Professionalism and Boundaries: Maintaining proper boundaries is vital for a healthy therapeutic partnership. Therapists should have clear policies and procedures governing confidentiality, scope of practice, and ethical values. Clients feel safer and more predictable when their behavior is consistent and professional.

Recognize that each client is unique, and that therapy approaches may need to be customized accordingly. Adjusting therapeutic procedures, interventions, and communication styles to match the client's particular requirements is what flexibility entails. Adapting to changing conditions and input from clients indicates attentiveness and fosters resilience in the therapeutic interaction.

Therapist and self-care To be effective in their roles, therapists must emphasize self-care and maintain their own well-being. Burnout and compassion fatigue can have an adverse effect on therapeutic partnerships. Therapists can maintain their resilience and provide consistent support to their clients by attending to their own physical, emotional, and psychological needs.

Continuous Learning and Professional Development: Therapists should participate in professional development programs and engage in continual learning. Extending knowledge and polishing abilities improves therapists' competency and ability to meet the changing requirements of their clients.

Remember that developing resilient therapy connections is a continuous and dynamic process. It necessitates dedication, self-reflection, and a willingness to adapt to each client's individual requirements and circumstances.

Transformational Tools: Therapeutic Approaches and Techniques

Therapeutic approaches and strategies include a wide spectrum of transformational instruments. CBT is a type of treatment that focuses on modifying cognitive patterns and behaviors. Emotional regulation and interpersonal skills are taught in dialectical behavior therapy (DBT). Mindfulness-based techniques promote awareness of the present moment. Traumatic memories are targeted via Eye Movement Desensitization and Reprocessing (EMDR). Psychodynamic treatment investigates unconscious processes and past events. Acceptance and Commitment Therapy (ACT) encourages the acceptance of challenging emotions as well as values-based action. In therapeutic contexts, these techniques, among others, provide avenues to personal growth, healing, and good transformation.

Cultural Awareness and Sensitivity

Cultural competency and sensitivity are critical characteristics for therapists. Being culturally competent entails learning and appreciating clients' varied backgrounds and views. It entails actively pursuing knowledge about various cultures and being able to modify therapy procedures to meet the requirements of individuals. Sensitivity, on the other hand, requires being aware of potential power imbalances, biases, and cultural misunderstandings during therapy. Therapists can establish a safe and inclusive setting for clients by cultivating cultural competency and sensitivity, encouraging trust, understanding, and good therapy outcomes.

Ethical considerations and boundaries

Understanding and respecting limits is critical for therapists in order to sustain a strong therapeutic relationship. Boundaries are the limitations and rules established by both the therapist and the client in order to maintain a safe and professional atmosphere. To maintain ethical standards, therapists must establish clear limits about confidentiality, dual partnerships, physical touch, and personal disclosure. Respecting these boundaries contributes to the creation of a safe and understandable environment for clients. Therapists must also handle ethical issues such as informed consent, cultural sensitivity, and avoiding injury. Maintaining these ethical principles ensures that therapy remains a beneficial and ethical practice that prioritizes clients' well-being.

CHAPTER 6

Life Improvement

Therapists have the extraordinary potential to transform people's lives via their knowledge and sensitivity. Empower individuals to navigate their emotions, heal wounds, and build healthy views via deep insight and assistance. Therapists assist clients discover their inner power by offering a safe space, helping them to overcome problems and discover new routes. Therapists are always being reinvented as they work to change people's lives. Each therapy contact provides essential insights that shape their own development and understanding of human nature. Therapists and their clients go on a path of personal and professional growth as a result of this reciprocal process, causing a beneficial ripple effect.

From Despair to Recovery

A therapist has the ability to turn despondency into healing. They listen, affirm, and comprehend the sorrow by providing compassionate guidance and a safe space. They promote connection through empathy, instilling a sense of belonging and merit. You must provide skills and tactics for navigating hardship, allowing people to uncover their inner strength and perseverance. Therapists assist in redefining negative attitudes and develop hope by addressing underlying beliefs and patterns. Their steadfast support and conviction in the client's ability to grow illuminate a road to healing, restoring hope where it had appeared gone.

Relationship Reconstruction

This is accomplished by providing a safe and impartial environment in which people or couples can express themselves. offer ideas and resources to improve communication, manage problems, and establish trust. Therapists help clients acquire insight into their own patterns and emotions through empathy and active listening, fostering healing and developing stronger connections within the partnership.

Reclaiming Life and Overcoming Trauma

Therapists play an important role in assisting clients in overcoming trauma and reclaiming their lives. They foster a judgment-free environment in which clients can examine and process their traumatic experiences. Therapists assist clients comprehend the impact of trauma on their thoughts, feelings, and actions by using evidence-based treatments such as trauma-focused therapy. They help clients establish appropriate coping techniques, increase resilience, and promote self-care. Therapists help people recover, grow, and take control of their lives by addressing the underlying impacts of trauma.

Personal Development and Resilience

To improve their professional performance, therapists should actively pursue personal growth and resilience. Therapists can obtain a deeper knowledge of their own emotions, prejudices, and triggers by engaging in self-reflection and personal development, allowing them to provide more empathic and non-judgmental assistance to their clients. Furthermore, personal development encourages continuous learning, allowing therapists to stay current on the newest research and therapeutic practices. Cultivating resilience is also important because it prepares therapists to withstand the emotional demands of their jobs, navigate difficult client situations, and recover from setbacks. Personal development and resilience are required for therapists in order to give effective and compassionate care to their clients.

Financial advantages are a crucial component of becoming a competent therapist. It is your unique and real characteristic that distinguishes you and makes others prefer you over others. While financial rewards are important, they should not overwhelm the various other benefits of working as a qualified therapist.

Clients are eager to pay any sum you mention when they appreciate the intrinsic value you deliver. This demonstrates their faith and belief in your talents. However, keep in mind that not everyone will be able to afford your fees. In such instances, your empathy should come into play, allowing you to be flexible and accommodating to individuals who cannot pay the full sum.

One of the amazing things about becoming a therapist is that you can work in any country, with people from all walks of life, and in a variety of organizations. There are wealthy people who appear to have everything yet are nevertheless suffering difficulties or problems. Building ties with such people can be beneficial because they regard you as a friend and confidant because of the help you provide.

Although financial gain is vital, it is not the most crucial component of being a competent therapist. Instead, concentrate on the exceptional skills and genuine care you offer to your profession, as well as the rewards that go beyond monetary recompense. Then comes the financial breakthrough.

Conclusion

Thus far, so good.

Thank you for sticking with me this far. In "The Therapist Triumph," we've taken a remarkable trip through the intricate workings of the human mind and the transformational potential of therapy. With each page turn, we have observed the protagonist's transformation from a shattered individual to a resilient, self-aware being. This narrative reminds us that healing is a slow process fraught with obstacles and uncertainties. It also highlights the unwavering strength of the human spirit and the extraordinary capacity for personal progress. As we say our goodbyes to these individuals, we are left with a renewed sense of optimism, knowing that everyone of us has the potential to triumph over our darkest problems.

Acknowledgments
I'd want to convey my heartfelt thanks to God Almighty for assisting me in making this book a success. To my family and friends, thank you for your steadfast love and understanding. And to my readers, thank you for joining me on this trip.